WORLD WINDOWS
Land and Water

HEINLE
CENGAGE Learning™

Y|S|G
A YBM COMPANY

Young & Son
Global, Inc.

Do you live closer to a mountain or an ocean?

Contents

plain

hill

mountain

lake

river

ocean

The Earth

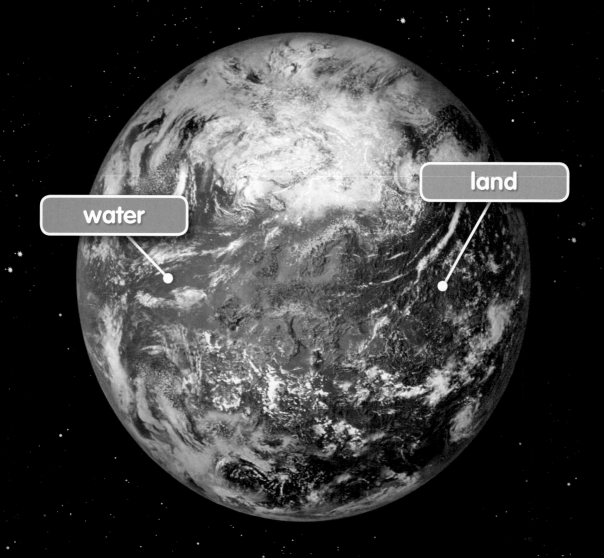

water

land

Look at the Earth!
The blue parts are water.
The green and brown parts are land.
There are different kinds of landforms
and bodies of water on Earth.

South Dakota, U.S.A.

Plain

A plain is a large, flat area of land.
Plains are often grassy.
Some plains are good for farming.

Cumbria, England

Hill

A hill is land that is higher than the land around it.
Most hills have round tops.

The Himalayas, Nepal

Mountain

Mountains are much higher than hills. They are the highest kind of land on Earth. Mountains are often steep and rocky.

Peyto Lake, Canada

Lake

A lake is a body of water that has land on all sides.

Most lakes have fresh water.

Kitka River, Finland

River

A river is a long body of fresh water.
Rivers carry water across the land.
They flow into lakes, other rivers, or oceans.

The Atlantic Ocean

Ocean

An ocean is the largest body of water.
Unlike most lakes and rivers, oceans
are made of salt water.
Oceans cover most of the Earth.

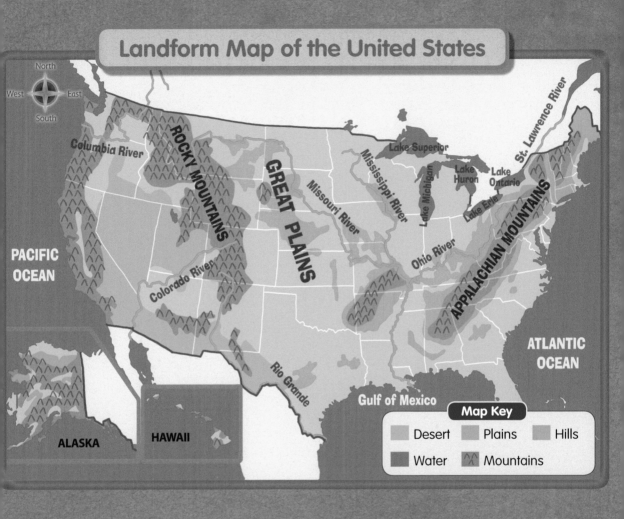

Landform Map of the United States

North
West • East
South

Columbia River

ROCKY MOUNTAINS

GREAT PLAINS

Missouri River

Mississippi River

Lake Superior

Lake Michigan

Lake Huron

Lake Ontario

Lake Erie

St. Lawrence River

APPALACHIAN MOUNTAINS

PACIFIC OCEAN

Colorado River

Ohio River

ATLANTIC OCEAN

Rio Grande

Gulf of Mexico

ALASKA

HAWAII

Map Key

Desert   Plains   Hills

Water   ⋀⋀ Mountains

The Earth's surface is different from place to place.

What are these types of land and water?

Read a Landform Map

A **landform map** uses colors and symbols to show different kinds of land.

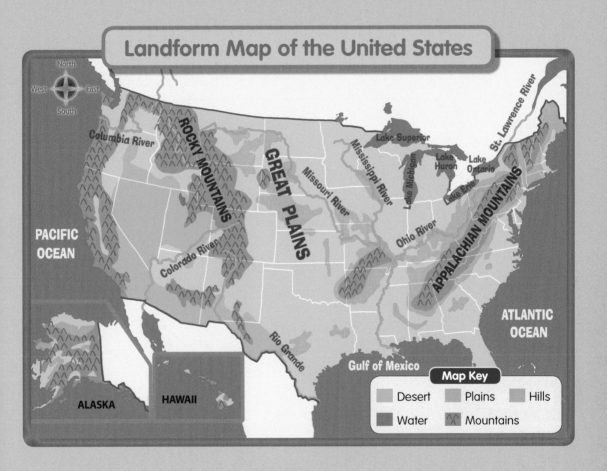

Landform Map of the United States

1. What does the orange part show?

2. What kinds of landforms are there in Alaska?

3. Are there more plains or mountains in the United States?

Glossary

flow
To move smoothly and continuously in one direction

fresh water
Water in lakes and rivers that does not contain any salt

rocky
Made of rock and therefore usually rough and difficult to travel along

steep
Rising or falling sharply

surface
The top layer or outside part of something

Index